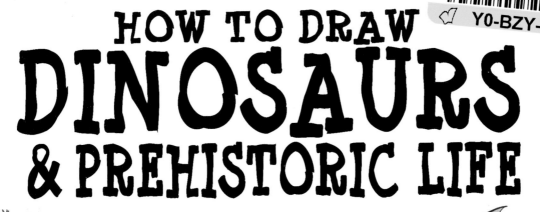

HOW TO DRAW
DINOSAURS
& PREHISTORIC LIFE

Marit Claridge
Consultant: John Shackell
Edited by Judy Tatchell

Designed by Mike Pringle and Richard Johnson

Illustrated by Val Biro, Philip Hood
and John Shackell

Y0-BZY-338

Contents

2	About this book	20	Cave paintings
4	Shapes and colors	21	Changing faces
6	Heads and tails	22	Dinosaur strip cartoons
8	A vegetarian giant	24	Cartoon lettering
10	Sea monsters	25	Moving pictures
12	Flying creatures	26	Ice Age mammals
14	Dinosaur characters	28	Fierce and meek animals
16	More dinosaur characters	30	Dinosaur stencils
18	Cave people	32	Index

About this book

Millions of years ago, monstrous dinosaurs and strange mammals ruled the earth. They are fun to draw because although there are some clues to what they looked like, nobody can be exactly sure.

Drawing around skeletons

Dinosaurs died out millions of years before humans appeared. The only clues to how they looked come from parts of their skeletons which have been found preserved in rock. These remains are called fossils. People called paleontologists piece the fossils together, working out how the missing bits of skeleton might have looked.

Look for pictures of dinosaur skeletons in books, which you can trace around, as shown here. Remember to leave space for the missing muscles and flesh.

Small bones are supported by small muscles, so the outline is close to the bones here.

Big bones need strong muscles to support them, so leave plenty of space for muscle here.

Coloring dinosaurs

Nobody knows exactly what colors the dinosaurs were. Most were probably similar to the trees and ferns around them.

Paleontologists base their color guesses on the reptiles and plants alive today. You, however, can color them as brightly as you wish.

Drawing styles

In this book you can find out how to draw realistic-looking prehistoric animals as well as cartoon characters. You can also find out how to draw cartoon cave people.

Dinosaurs and cave people often appear together in cartoons even though dinosaurs died out long before cave people appeared.

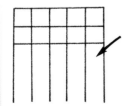

Scaling up

You can learn a lot about how to draw prehistoric life by copying the illustrations in this book. If you want to make your drawing bigger than the one in the book, you can scale up the illustration using a grid.

Draw a grid on tracing paper made up of equal-sized squares.

Put the grid over the picture you want to copy.

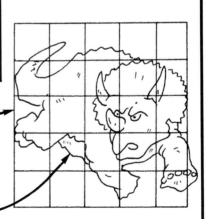

Draw another light pencil grid on a piece of drawing paper. Use the same number of squares but twice the size of those on the tracing grid, to double the size of the picture.

Look at the squares laid on top of the picture. Copy the shapes in each one into the same square on the drawing paper grid.

Erase the grid lines when you have inked the outline.

Shapes and colors

On these two pages there are tips on how to draw and color prehistoric animals. You may find these techniques useful later in the book.

Simple shapes

Prehistoric deer

1

2

3

However complicated an animal looks, it is made up of simpler shapes. Throughout the book there are line drawings that show how to build up the animals using simple shapes. Draw the red lines first, then the blue and then the green.

Colors

Many of the animals in the book are colored using watercolor paints. Some of the colors have unusual names. These are explained in **Artist's colors** boxes.

A paintbox with a large range of colors should have all the colors you need. You can also buy tubes of watercolors in any color you wish.

Artist's colors
Ochre is a pale brownish yellow.

Washes

A wash is a thin coat of watery paint. When you color a large animal, mix up plenty of the wash color in a separate container.

Skin textures

Dinosaurs had thick, leathery skins like elephants, or dry, warty skins. You can use the tips below to paint and color the skins of the dinosaurs in this book.

Dry, warty skin

Color the area with a light to medium wash. When dry, add a second, darker layer to the shaded areas.

Cover the area with thick white spots. Mix some wash color with the white to darken the spots in the shaded areas.

Add dark shadows beneath the spots and draw extra dark lines beneath the body to strengthen the shadows.

Using a sponge

Thick, leathery skin

  or

For another warty skin, begin with a wash, as before. Then dip a small sponge in a darker mix of paint and dab it gently over the area.

Begin with a background wash. When dry, draw dark, heavy lines where the body creases. Add highlights with dry, white paint.

With crayons and pencils, color the dinosaur with the paper resting on a rough surface, such as sandpaper, cement or grainy wood.

Artist's tip

Some of the prehistoric creatures in this book are two-legged. A common problem when drawing them is that they can look off balance. This makes them appear weak.

To make them balance, there must be as much weight in front of their legs as behind. Draw a vertical line and build your animal up around it.

Weight too far back.

Weight too far forward.

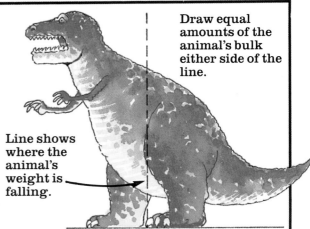

Line shows where the animal's weight is falling.

Draw equal amounts of the animal's bulk either side of the line.

Heads and tails

The dinosaurs on these two pages have strange heads or tails and odd bodies. These make them fun to draw and ideal for turning into cartoons.

Stegosaurus

Use a darker shade for the far plates and far legs. This makes them look further away.

Plates

The head hangs low as the front legs are shorter than the back legs.

Sketch the basic shape of the Stegosaurus (pronounced Steg-oh-saw-rus) in pencil. Begin with the body, then add the neck, head, tail and legs. Draw the plates last.

To color the Stegosaurus, use the techniques shown on page 5 for dry warty skin on the body and thick leathery skin around the legs.

Ankylosaurus

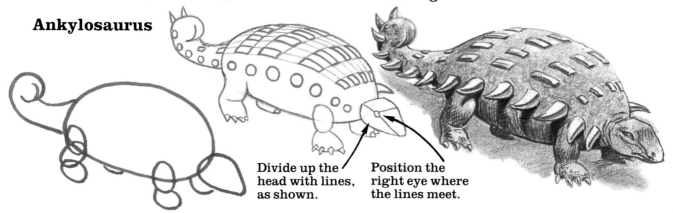

Divide up the head with lines, as shown.

Position the right eye where the lines meet.

Above are the basic shapes for an Ankylosaurus (pronounced An-kil-oh-saw-rus).

Draw faint circles along the body to position the body spikes and curved lines to position the back plates.

Add spikes and back plates. Leave white highlights on them. Add strong shadows under the spikes and body.

Crested dinosaurs

Some dinosaurs had crests on their heads which probably helped them recognize each other. The crests had air passages inside which meant the dinosaurs could make loud, bellowing calls. These crests may have been very colorful.

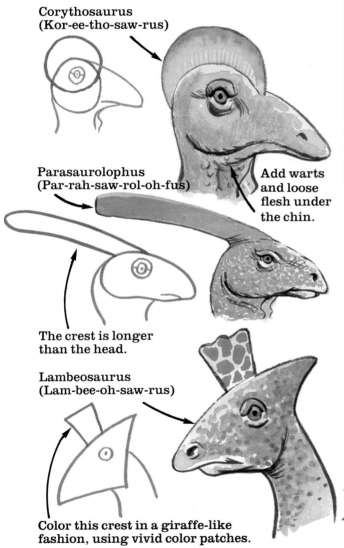

Corythosaurus
(Kor-ee-tho-saw-rus)

Parasaurolophus
(Par-rah-saw-rol-oh-fus)

Add warts and loose flesh under the chin.

The crest is longer than the head.

Lambeosaurus
(Lam-bee-oh-saw-rus)

Color this crest in a giraffe-like fashion, using vivid color patches.

Cartoon dinosaurs

The Ankylosaurus used the bone at the end of its tail as a club to fend off meat-eaters. Try copying this cartoon which makes fun of the situation.

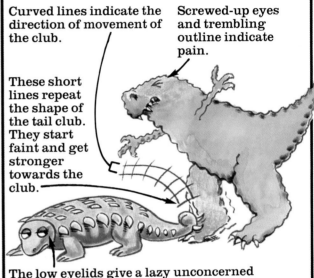

Curved lines indicate the direction of movement of the club.

Screwed-up eyes and trembling outline indicate pain.

These short lines repeat the shape of the tail club. They start faint and get stronger towards the club.

The low eyelids give a lazy unconcerned look.

Make your own monster

You could try mixing up some of the heads, tails and bodies on these pages to make your own imaginary monster.

A vegetarian giant

The Diplodocus (Dip-loh-doh-kus) was the longest dinosaur. It measured 90ft from its nose to the tip of its tail — about as long as a tennis court.

Use a darker, thicker mix of the wash color for the shadows under the body.

Wrinkles

Draw in wrinkles around the legs and where the tail and neck bend.

Color the far legs a darker shade.

Shade under the body and neck and in the curve of the tail.

Draw the oval body shape first. Then add the long neck and tail and the heavy legs.

The Diplodocus had thick, leathery skin, like an elephant. Color it with shades of green watercolor using the technique shown on page 5.

Turn your animal around

A simple plasticine* model can be a great help if you want to draw your Diplodocus from different angles.

Mold some plasticine* into seven pieces — the body, neck, tail and four legs. Press the pieces together to form your model. Keep it small or the neck will be too heavy to stand out from the body. You could stand the model on a small piece of cardboard so that you can move it easily.

Shadows on the body help to make the animal look heavy and solid. Shine a lamp or flashlight at your model so that you can see where the shadows fall.

*Plastic modeling clay

In the swamp

The Diplodocus lived in swamps. Try drawing a wet, glossy Diplodocus in a prehistoric swamp.

Paint simple leaf shapes.

Less detail in distant trees.

White highlights make the skin look wet.

Use darker shades below.

Steam rising.

Let colors run together.

Keep near edges sharp.

Use muddy browns for the water.

Add touches of blue to reflect the sky.

Get a swampy water effect by taking wiggly lines from roots and stems.

Draw the outline of the Diplodocus and tree trunks in pencil. Paint ferns and trees with plenty of vines. Color the trees and water with very wet washes. While the paint is still damp, dab some of the color away with tissue. This gives the effect of steam rising. Color the Diplodocus as before.

A worm's eye view

In this unusual view of a Diplodocus, its tiny head is drawn as big as its body. This makes the head seem close while the body disappears behind. Try drawing this cartoon, following the tips for making the body recede into the background.

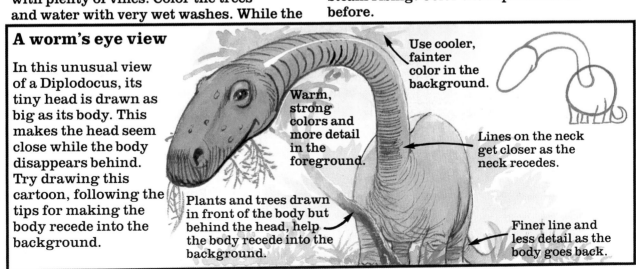

Use cooler, fainter color in the background.

Warm, strong colors and more detail in the foreground.

Lines on the neck get closer as the neck recedes.

Plants and trees drawn in front of the body but behind the head, help the body recede into the background.

Finer line and less detail as the body goes back.

Sea monsters

At the time of the dinosaurs, the seas were the home of huge creatures. These two pages show you how to draw three sea monsters in a dramatic scene above and below the water.

Indigo fades to pale yellow underneath.

Add white highlights for a glossy wet skin.

For sharp-looking teeth, draw a row of triangles. Paint them white against a dark mouth.

Fade the sea color and draw the waves smaller and fainter towards the horizon. This helps make the distant sea look further away.

Draw a sharp outline above the water.

Ichthyosaurus
(Ik-thi-oh-saw-rus)

Artist's colors

Indigo is a very dark blue.

Outline fades underwater. Blend with sea water color.

Elasmosaurus
(Ee-laz-mo-saw-rus)

Animal shapes

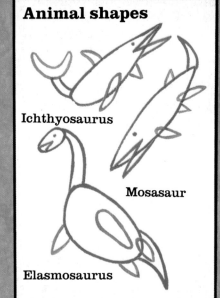

Ichthyosaurus

Mosasaur

Elasmosaurus

Scaly skin

The Mosasaur has scaly skin, like a crocodile. Use a wash of greeny browns and grays. When the paint is dry, use a thin brush, sharp crayon or a fine dark felt tip to draw the scaly ridges. Add white highlights to make it look wet and shiny.

Long white highlight makes fish look wet.

For fish, use shades of blue, green and yellow. Start dark at the top and fade to pale yellow beneath. Criss-cross with fine black lines.

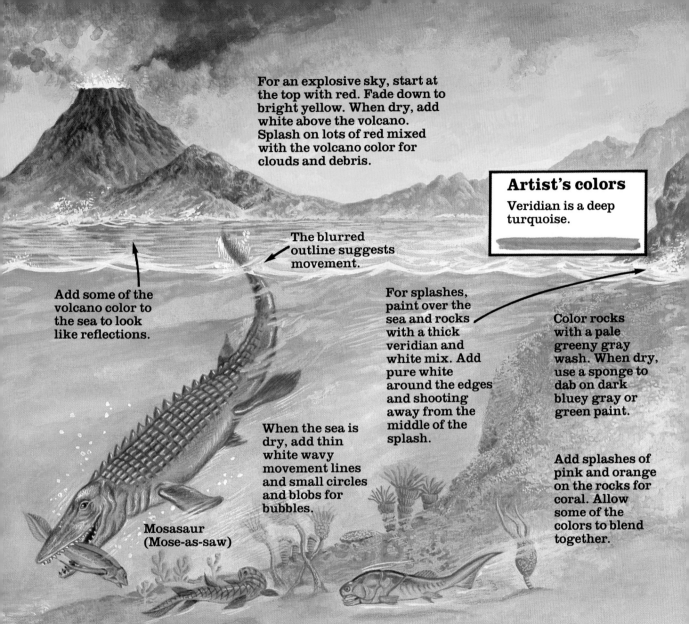

For an explosive sky, start at the top with red. Fade down to bright yellow. When dry, add white above the volcano. Splash on lots of red mixed with the volcano color for clouds and debris.

Artist's colors

Veridian is a deep turquoise.

The blurred outline suggests movement.

Add some of the volcano color to the sea to look like reflections.

For splashes, paint over the sea and rocks with a thick veridian and white mix. Add pure white around the edges and shooting away from the middle of the splash.

Color rocks with a pale greeny gray wash. When dry, use a sponge to dab on dark bluey gray or green paint.

When the sea is dry, add thin white wavy movement lines and small circles and blobs for bubbles.

Add splashes of pink and orange on the rocks for coral. Allow some of the colors to blend together.

Mosasaur (Mose-as-saw)

Under the sea

First color the monsters, coral and underwater rocks. Leave these to dry. Then cover the whole area with a veridian wash. When this dries, add wavy lines of darker veridian across the picture. Paint darker veridian lines alongside the Mosasaur too. These help to make the creature look as if it is moving through the sea.

11

Flying creatures

Above the dinosaurs the skies were ruled by large flying reptiles, called pterosaurs. Here you can find out how to draw two different types as well as a strip cartoon about an Archaeopteryx, the first real bird.

Paint the Pteranodon (Ter-a-no-don) with a thin grey wash. When dry, go over it again with a thin pinky brown wash.

Pteranodon

Draw a faint dotted line and use this to position the body, legs and arms. Add the wings, neck and head.

Add shadows and veins in dark brown.

Use a thick mix of the pinky brown color for highlights.

Follow the tips on page 10 and 11 for coloring the sea and rocks.

Artist's tip

You can save time by using a hairdrier to dry the wash.

Archaeopteryx

The Archaeopteryx (Ark-ee-op-ter-iks) used its sharp claws to climb trees and its wings to glide. It was too heavy to fly and its beak full of teeth would have made it nose-heavy.

Try copying this strip cartoon about an Archaeopteryx.

Beads of sweat show effort.

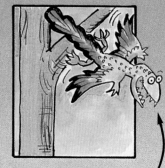

Draw the outline and feathers in black felt tip. Color the bird with bright crayons or felt tips.

Wide eyes, curved brows and gaping mouth suggest mounting panic.

Bird's eye view

Animals and trees look quite different from above. The parts of the body that are closer to you look bigger than those that are further away.

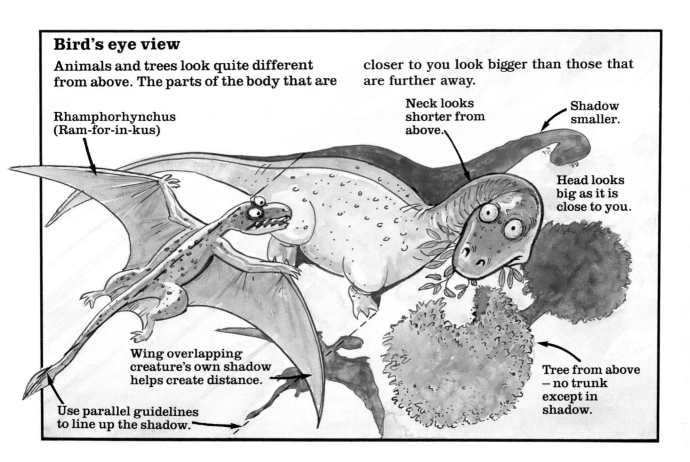

Rhamphorhynchus
(Ram-for-in-kus)

Neck looks shorter from above.

Shadow smaller.

Head looks big as it is close to you.

Wing overlapping creature's own shadow helps create distance.

Use parallel guidelines to line up the shadow.

Tree from above – no trunk except in shadow.

Lines show direction of movement

CRUNCH

Radiating lines make the impact look more dramatic.

Extra beads of sweat suggest greater effort.

Dinosaur characters

People write stories about dinosaurs and prehistoric times because of the excitement of the unknown. All that remains of these creatures are their skeletons. The rest has to be made up. This mixture of reality and fantasy makes them ideal subjects for stories.

The dinosaurs on the next four pages are drawn in a cartoon story-book style. They are given characters, like people in a story.

Tyrannosaurus rex

The Tyrannosaurus rex (Tie-ran-oh-saw-rus rex) or T.rex was the biggest meat eater that ever lived. Its head alone was 5 feet long — big enough to swallow a man whole.

Try painting the fierce T.rex below using masking fluid* to give its colorful skin a bumpy texture. You can also use this technique for the Triceratops on the next page and other dinosaurs with scaly skin.

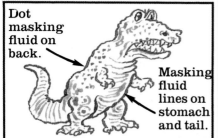

Dot masking fluid on back.

Masking fluid lines on stomach and tail.

Copy or trace the T.rex. Paint on the masking fluid with a paper clip — do not use a brush or you will ruin it.

Green for back.

Yellow and orange for stomach.

When the masking fluid is dry, color in the T.rex with watercolor.

White marks left behind by masking fluid.

When dry, rub off the masking fluid with your fingers. This will leave white marks.

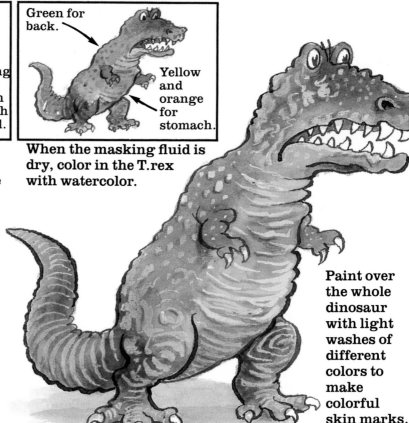

Paint over the whole dinosaur with light washes of different colors to make colorful skin marks.

*You can buy masking fluid from art material shops.

Triceratops

This brave, charging Triceratops (Try-ser-a-tops) was a fierce, plant-eating dinosaur. Its huge frilled head, three horns and strange beaked mouth help to give it a lot of character. Trace or copy the Triceratops here and color it with orange, yellow and brown watercolor.

Add extra, soft markings with colored crayons.

A timid T. rex

In most pictures the T. rex is shown as terrible and frightening. This T. rex is given a timid character. It looks alarmed — as it may have been if charged at by the heavily armored Triceratops.

The down-turned mouth and backward looking eyes give the T. rex a worried expression.

Here it is running away. The staring eyes, slightly opened mouth and turned head make it look even more alarmed than before.

More dinosaur characters

The dinosaurs in this prehistoric scene are running from a fierce Tyrannosaurus rex. The artist makes the most of each dinosaur's special features to give the characters extra life. Copy the characters and try to change the expressions around using the tips given here.

The Diplodocus would have had little defense against the T.rex. Her dilated, turned-back eyes and down-turned mouth make the Diplodocus look frightened.

The frowning eyes and down-turned mouth make this Ankylosaurus look angry at being chased.

Color the prehistoric
landscape with soft
watercolors and crayons. Use
a pen to outline shapes on trees
and bushes.

Your dinosaurs can be as
colorful as you like. Use
bright yellow, orange, purple,
green, brown and blue to keep
the character from looking
drab.

The Rhamphorhynchus
could fly away from
danger. It looks happy
with an open mouth and
big smile.

The Parasaurolophus was
probably a fast runner. Closed
eyes and a slight smile make
him look
confident.

The Stegosaurus probably
moved slowly. Wide eyes
and a slightly opened mouth
make it look worried.

17

Cave people

On these two pages you can see how to draw a family of cave people.

Caveman and woman

Use the same basic shape for both the caveman and cavewoman.

Divide head into quarters to position eyes, nose and mouth.

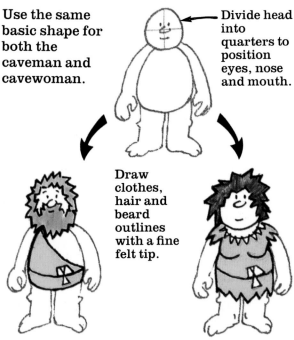

Draw clothes, hair and beard outlines with a fine felt tip.

Color the clothes with a yellow marker. Use a brown marker for the spots.

Jagged line looks like a tooth necklace.

A touch of gray on lower edge of ax head makes ax look more solid.

Add hairy arms and legs with a pencil.

Cave children

Use a pear shaped body for a boy or girl.

Divide head into equal quarters to position eyes and nose.

Thinner arms and legs than for adults.

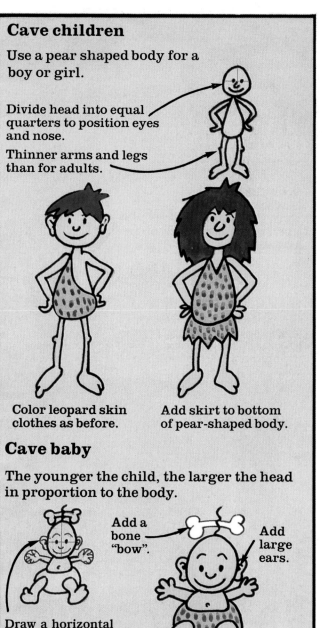

Color leopard skin clothes as before.

Add skirt to bottom of pear-shaped body.

Cave baby

The younger the child, the larger the head in proportion to the body.

Add a bone "bow".

Add large ears.

Draw a horizontal line below halfway down the head to position eyes.

Turning around

You can use the same basic body shapes to draw the cave children and adults from the front, back and side.

For a back view, turn feet away and fill head completely with hair color.

For a three-quarter view, move facial features to left or right. Add the nose in profile. Change the arms and legs as shown.

The side-on caveman in this cartoon is drawn starting with the same body shape as for a front view. You only have to alter the arm and leg positions and draw the face in profile.

Here you can see how coloring just the relevant part of the picture makes the point of the joke stand out.

Cave family at home

This cartoon shows some tricks you can use to make your pictures lively.

Leg breaks out to give impression of running into the picture.

Lines repeat tail shape.

For the blotchy effect, apply the paint with a sponge. Add more paint with a brush in darker areas.

Clouds of dust help to show speed.

Dust where ball bounces.

Cave paintings

Cave people painted pictures of animals such as horses and bison on the walls of their caves. The paintings on this page are copies of real cave paintings.

Copy the shapes and follow the coloring tips for realistic looking cave paintings.

The wall

You can achieve a realistic looking rock wall by putting a sheet of rough sandpaper under your paper. Color the wall by rubbing fairly hard with crayons or pastels. The wall on the right is colored in this way.

You can also use watercolors, as in the rest of the page. Use watery washes of soft colors. Apply the colors in patches, adding extra paint between the patches to create angles.

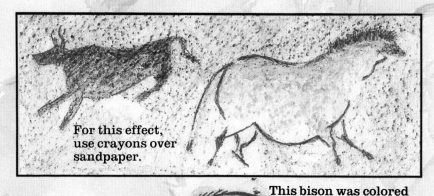

For this effect, use crayons over sandpaper.

Colors

Cave people ground down soft colored rocks to make their paints. They would have used colors like the ones below.

Yellow   Yellow ochre   Red ochre   Raw sienna   Burnt sienna

Burnt umber   Black   Grays   White

This bison was colored with paint dabbed on with a finger.

Pick out horns in white.

Use a few single brush strokes for the horse.

Changing faces

Cartoons are often made funny by the expressions on the characters' faces.

There are tips on how to draw different expressions throughout the book. Here are some more for you to practice.

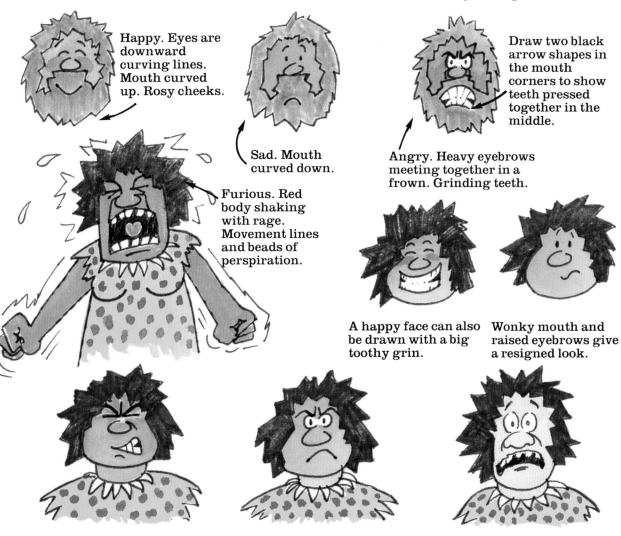

Happy. Eyes are downward curving lines. Mouth curved up. Rosy cheeks.

Sad. Mouth curved down.

Draw two black arrow shapes in the mouth corners to show teeth pressed together in the middle.

Angry. Heavy eyebrows meeting together in a frown. Grinding teeth.

Furious. Red body shaking with rage. Movement lines and beads of perspiration.

A happy face can also be drawn with a big toothy grin.

Wonky mouth and raised eyebrows give a resigned look.

Pain. Eyes screwed up tight. Red face. Mouth open one side only showing grinding teeth.

Downturned mouth and frowning eyes give a displeased expression.

Frightened. A green face with wide staring eyes, raised eyebrows and a quaking mouth.

Dinosaur strip cartoons

A strip cartoon is a funny story told in more than one picture. Each picture is within a frame with speech and thought added in bubbles. Try to make your characters look the same in each frame. It helps if you give them distinct features such as a big nose or beard.

Artist's tip

You can turn the characters of your strip cartoon around with the help of tracing paper. This works for side-views and three-quarter views. Trace the figure and simply turn the tracing over for the opposite view.

The tracing is like a mirror image where everything is reversed. If your character has clothes off one shoulder or a club in one hand, this has to be reversed back again.

Speech bubbles

You can add speech and thought to your story in bubbles. Use capital letters and keep the speech short. You can also add sound effects, which you can find out about on page 24.

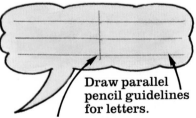

Draw parallel pencil guidelines for letters.

To center the lettering, draw a vertical line. Then put the same number of words on each side (count the spaces between words as one letter).

Use small lettering in a large bubble for quiet speech.

For loud speech, do the opposite.

A line of small circles from the bubble indicates thought.

With more than one speech bubble in a frame, people will read them from the top left corner down to the bottom right corner. Make sure you place them in the order you want them read.

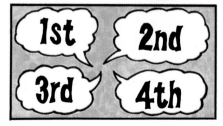

Framing

Use the tips below to vary the size and shape of the
picture frames. This makes the strip look more interesting.

Different sized boxes.

Use a circle to highlight a particular moment.

Use a series of zs to show someone or something asleep.

Dinosaur goes over three frames for a before-and-after sequence.

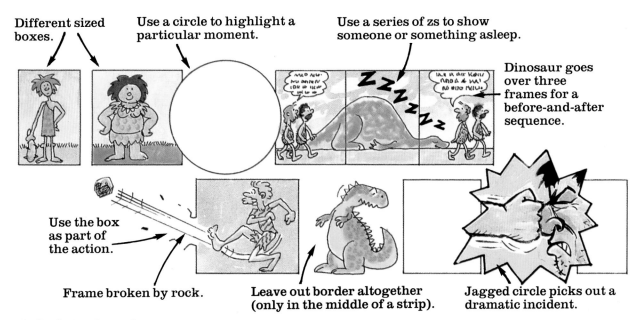

Use the box as part of the action.

Frame broken by rock.

Leave out border altogether (only in the middle of a strip).

Jagged circle picks out a dramatic incident.

A finished strip

This strip cartoon uses some of the techniques described.
There are also some more tips for you to follow.

Flash breaking out of frame gives a dramatic effect.

Add extra letters for a long scream.

Hint of smoke leads to next frame.

Movement lines indicate head turning quickly.

Circle broken by elbow.

A close-up varies the look of the pictures.

Different sized frames.

Action continues beyond the last frame.

Cartoon lettering

You can make dramatic sound effects for your cartoons. Use colors and shapes that suggest the sound you want to make. Try drawing the words on this page and then use the tips to make up your own words.

The wiggly outlines of the letters make them look as if they have been squashed by the dinosaur's tail.

Draw soft, squelchy letter shapes.

The extra letters give the impression of a long noise. The letters get bigger and bigger to suggest a loud growl.

Drop shadows

You can make the sound have more impact by adding a drop shadow. Use sharp letter angles to suggest a loud sound.

Draw the letter outlines, then trace them on to tracing paper. Use the tracing to draw the shadow under and to the right of the original word.

Black in the shadow. You can also try using colored letters and shadows.

Extra dimensions

In this example, the word radiates out from the crashing caveman. This helps to give a three-dimensional effect.

Draw the caveman. Mark a point in the center of his body and draw pencil guidelines radiating out from this point.

Use the guidelines to draw the letters.

Add impact lines last.

Moving pictures

For fast-action cartoons there are simple ways to make your characters look as if they are on the run. The two main ways to draw fast running legs are shown in the cartoon below.

Lines around the body suggest movement.

Beads of perspiration.

Leg positions

Horizontal lines add to the speed effect.

Movement lines

Draw feet clear of ground.

The dinosaur's legs are a blurred spiral of lines. The foot shape is repeated again and again around the edge.

The caveman's legs have movement lines to show that he is running. In both methods the feet are clear of the ground.

Movement and distance

Add giant prehistoric ferns. Draw them large in the foreground and smaller as you go into the distance.

Draw figures in the foreground larger than those further away.

Fade the sky color towards the horizon.

Dust disappears.

Here, dust kicked up by the runners helps to give the impression of movement. Draw the dust clouds smaller as they disappear out of view to give depth to the cartoon.

Ice Age mammals

The earth became very cold in the Ice Ages. Huge sheets of ice spread out from the North and South Poles. Prehistoric mammals in the northern continents had to move south or adapt to the cold. The mammoth, woolly rhinoceros and cave bear had woolly coats to help them survive in the cold.

Woolly rhinoceros

The woolly rhino would have used its large horn to dig up plants.

Color the whole body with a light brownish ochre wash. Build up the woolly coat by using short brush strokes of dark brown.

Add black brush strokes for extra shadows.

Use dark gray on a pale wash for this wrinkly skin.

Artist's colors

Ochre is a pale brownish yellow.

Cave bear

The prehistoric cave bear was about 13 feet tall on its hind legs — over a third bigger than modern brown bears. Make its coat look furry by building up layers of short brush strokes on a smooth pale layer of background color.

Color the bear lightly with a burnt sienna wash. Use darker tones of brown for the fur.

Artist's colors

Burnt sienna is a warm brown.

For a menacing snarl, add teeth with thick white paint against a red mouth.

A crisp, black outline on the claws makes them look sharp.

Mammoth

Mammoths probably used their long tusks to clear snow from plants to eat. Follow the tips below to draw a mammoth in a bleak, wintry scene.

Use cold colors for the sky. Begin with streaks of pale blue and yellow wash. Allow the colors to overlap. Add gray patches for the clouds.

Highlights make the mountains look three dimensional.

Dark shadows on the tusks make them stand out against the snow.

The snow reflects the sky colors. Use blues and grays for shadows. Add pale pink as well as yellow for highlights.

Color the mammoth with a burnt sienna wash. Add touches of gray over the brown to give a mottled effect. Then add dark brown mixed with indigo for the shadows.

Cartoon bear

Cartoons are often drawn with just a few, carefully placed lines. The cartoon below is done in this way, which gives it a fresh, lively look.

Caveman's face has no outline. Your eye fills in the missing detail.

Roots drawn as grasping claws add drama.

Fierce and meek animals

When the dinosaurs died out about 65 million years ago, mammals took over the world. Here you can find out how to draw the terrible saber tiger, a meek, armored glyptodon and a fierce meat-eating bird.

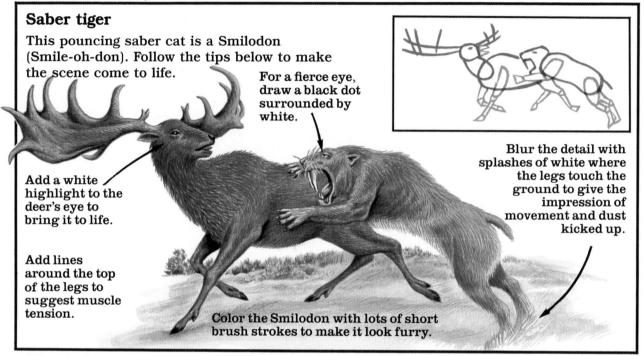

Saber tiger

This pouncing saber cat is a Smilodon (Smile-oh-don). Follow the tips below to make the scene come to life.

For a fierce eye, draw a black dot surrounded by white.

Add a white highlight to the deer's eye to bring it to life.

Add lines around the top of the legs to suggest muscle tension.

Color the Smilodon with lots of short brush strokes to make it look furry.

Blur the detail with splashes of white where the legs touch the ground to give the impression of movement and dust kicked up.

Glyptodon

In contrast to the Smilodon, the Glyptodon (Glip-toe-don) was a slow animal that ate insects, worms and berries. Its bony shell and spiky tail helped to protect it against meat eaters. Use lots of highlights on the shell to make it look shiny.

The contrast of highlights and shade helps the shell look rounded.

Add highlights to edges of spots facing the light.

Fine white lines on neck and underside look like fur.

Begin with a dark brown wash. Keep the paint lighter on the side where the light falls. Let it dry before adding the spots.

Use a mixture of white and ochre paint for the spots. Add more ochre to the mix for the shaded areas.

Diatryma

The flightless Diatryma (Die-ah-try-ma) was over 10 feet tall — nearly as tall as an African elephant. Use the tips on page five to help balance the bird.

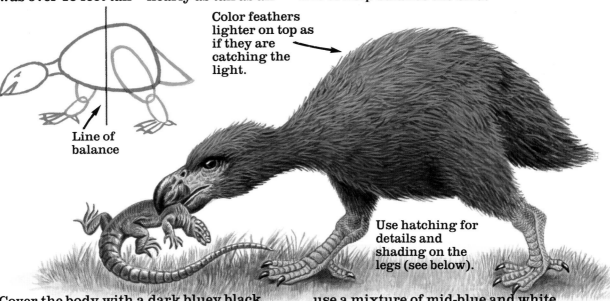

Line of balance

Color feathers lighter on top as if they are catching the light.

Use hatching for details and shading on the legs (see below).

Cover the body with a dark bluey black wash. When dry, add another layer to the underside for shadow. For the feathers, use a mixture of mid-blue and white. Apply the paint with short flicks of the brush in one direction only.

Cartoon Diatryma

The Diatryma was such a strange looking bird that you only need to simplify its shape slightly to draw this weird cartoon character. Use felt tips for bold coloring.

ANYBODY HOME?

KNOCK KNOCK

Artist's tip

Hatching
Hatching is a method of shading using a series of lines.

Cross-hatching
Use two sets of lines criss-crossing for darker shadows.

Multi-hatching
Continue adding lines in new directions to get the shading as dark as you want.

29

Dinosaur stencils

You can make a dinosaur stencil from thin cardboard - an empty cereal box will do. Carefully cut out the animal shape so that you can use both the positive and negative. The simpler the shape, the easier it is to cut. Use a pair of small, sharp scissors.

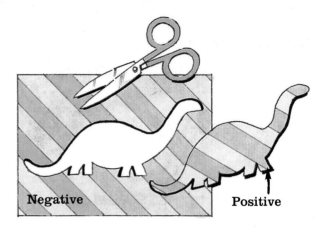

Negative

Positive

Candle wax textures

Candle wax resists paint and leaves interesting patterns. Use thin, white birthday candles. You could copy the diplodocus shape below to make a stencil.

Paint from side to center.

Hold down the negative stencil and cover it with a yellow wash. Use a fairly dry wash or it will seep under the stencil.

When dry, draw wrinkles and scaly patterns over the diplodocus with a candle.

Keep the stencil in place and paint all over the shape with a dark bluey green wash.

Paint plant silhouettes in a pale mauve wash. When dry, draw on stem and leaf shapes in candle wax. Finish with a dark mauve wash on top.

For this sky, paint the sun then cover it with wax. Draw lines and swirls in wax for clouds. Paint over the top with a pink wash fading to yellow.

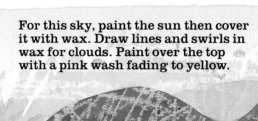

Apply lines of wax before adding the watercolor to look like reflections.

Artist's tip

Cover the dinosaur with the positive stencil when you color the background. This keeps the dinosaur clean.

Splatter method

This Diplodocus is colored by flicking paint off a toothbrush.

Lay down the negative stencil and apply a pale green wash. Let this dry.

Then dip a toothbrush into a darker mix of paint. Use your finger or the edge of a ruler to run along the bristles towards you, flicking the paint on to the Diplodocus.

Scratch out eye and mouth shape with a pin.

Add more splatters at the bottom for darker shadows.

Chalks and crayons

Reverse the stencil to turn the dinosaur around. This dinosaur is colored with crayons inside the negative stencil. There is no hard outline and the dinosaur is made to look rounded by the direction of the crayon lines.

Add eyes and mouth last with a soft pencil.

Curve the lines around the body.

Build up the body shape with crossing lines.

Use chalk on its side to make block shapes in the background.

Artist's tip

Use fixing spray to stop chalks from smudging. You can buy this from most art material stores.

31

Index

Ankylosaurus, 6,16
  cartoon, 7

balance, 5,29
bird's eye view, 13

cartoon lettering, 24
cartoon movement, 25
cave bear, 26
  cartoon, 27
cave paintings, 20
  bison, 20
  horse, 20
cave people, 18,19
  cave baby, 18,19
  cave children, 18,19
  caveman, 18,19
  cavewoman, 18
  expressions, 21
cave wall, 20
colors, 2,4,16,20
copying pictures, 3
crested dinosaurs, 7
  Corythosaurus, 7
  Lambeosaurus, 7
  Parasaurolophus, 7,17
cross-hatching, 29

deer, 4,28
Diatryma, 29
  cartoon, 29
dinosaurs, 6-9,13,14-17

dinosaur characters, 14-17
dinosaur skeletons, 2,3
dinosaur stencils, 30,31
Diplodocus, 8-9,16
  cartoon, 9,13
  plasticine model, 8

enlarging pictures, 3

fish, 10
flying creatures, 12-13
  Archaeopteryx,
    cartoon, 12,13
  Pteranodon, 12
  Rhamphorhynchus,
    13,17

Glyptodon, 28
  cartoon, 29

hatching, 29

imaginary monster, 7

mammals, 26-29
mammoth, 27
multi-hatching, 29

prehistoric landscapes,
  9,10-11,12,16-17
  dry, 16-17
  Ice Age, 27

rocks, 11,12
sea, 10-11,12
swamp, 9

saber tiger, 28
  Smilodon, 28
sea monsters, 10-11
  Elasmosaurus, 10
  Ichthyosaurus, 10
  Mosasaur, 10, 11
shadows, 8, 13
shapes, 4
skin textures, 5, 10
  bony shell, 28
  feathers, 29
  furry coat, 26, 27, 28
  leathery skin,
    5, 6, 8
  scales, 10
  warty skin, 5, 6, 14
Stegosaurus, 6, 17
strip cartoons, 12, 13, 22-23
  framing, 23
  speech bubbles, 22

Triceratops, 15
Tyrannosaurus rex,
  14,15,16

watercolor washes, 4
woolly rhinoceros, 26
worm's eye view 13